LEONARDO DA VINCI

LEONARDO DA VINCI

Hellmut Wohl

Boston University

McGRAW-HILL BOOK COMPANY · NEW YORK · LONDON · TORONTO · SYDNEY

Cover picture, *Study for the Madonna Litta,* detail (about 1480–1485), silverpoint on green prepared paper, Louvre, Paris. Photographs for Figures 1, 2, 5, and 10, courtesy Anderson-Art Reference Bureau. Photographs for Figures 3, 4, 8, and 12, courtesy Giraudon. Photographs for Figures 6, 7, 13, 16, 17, 18, 19 and 20, reproduced by gracious permission of Her Majesty Queen Elizabeth II.

The career of Leonardo da Vinci was a perfect embodiment of the Renaissance belief in man's power to shape his own destiny and to shape the world. He was born the illegitimate son of a Tuscan village notary and was said to have died in the arms of the King of France.

LEONARDO was the first artist who was the equal of princes and popes. (Michelangelo and Raphael were younger, Michelangelo by twenty-three years, Raphael by thirty-one). His achievements in art and science — which he and his age considered interrelated aspects of the striving to understand ourselves and the world around us — have influenced the way we see and think even today.

The pathos of Michelangelo and the grandeur of Raphael have had a greater hold on the imagination of men than the complexity of the genius of Leonardo. But he is a unique and legendary figure in our pantheon of great artists. No painting has ever exercised such magic as the *Mona Lisa,* and none has ingrained itself so deeply in our minds' eye as *The Last Supper.* Leonardo's paintings, like the smile of the *Mona Lisa,* move us in ways for which we cannot account except by recognizing that they touch the very mystery of life and creation. In Giorgio Vasari's *Lives* of Italian artists, written a half-century after the death of Leonardo, Vasari called him "divine"; and when Raphael painted the figure of Plato in the *School of Athens* in the Papal apartments in the Vatican, he gave him the features of Leonardo, as we know them from a *Self-portrait* that Leonardo drew some years later at the age of about sixty (Figure 1).

One of the most revealing images of Leonardo's time is the figure of God imparting life to the body of Adam, on the Sistine ceiling, painted by Michelangelo in 1510. Michelangelo's power and rhetoric were foreign and antipathetic to Leonardo ("There was no love lost between him and Michelangelo Buonarroti," Vasari wrote), and yet the meaning of this image transcends the antagonism and the temperamental differences between the two men. Through heroic human figures Michelangelo has expressed a truth which Leonardo also strove to formulate, in art and in science: the embodiment in man, nature, and art of an intelligible cosmic order.

Leonardo addressed himself to this task not like a theologian or a humanist but in the spirit of an empirical philosopher. "All our knowledge," he wrote in his *Notebooks,* "has its origin in our perceptions." He believed that visual art was the most comprehensive tool for understanding the universe. For centuries art had been the making of images. Beginning with Leonardo it also came to be a means for extending the horizon of men's awareness and insight. Great as his influence was on the classic style of the High Renaissance, of which he was the founder, it is insignificant compared with his importance in redirecting the

Figure 1.
[Facing title page]
Self-portrait (about 1514)
red chalk, 13⅛" x 7¼"
Royal Library, Turin

[Facing this page]
Detail of *The Deluge*
Figure 20, page 31

role of visual art. History has confirmed the position to which Raphael elevated him in the *School of Athens.*

Leonardo was not the first man who brought art and science together. In the early decades of the fifteenth century Renaissance art had begun to take shape in the hands of a number of Florentine artist-scientists. These men — the sculptors Donatello and Ghiberti, the architect Filippo Brunelleschi, and the painters Masaccio and Paolo Uccello — shared a belief in a new art in which the artist, as Leonardo was to say, "must act as the interpreter between nature and art, explaining through the latter the causes and effects of the former as they obey nature's proper law." For them, as for Leonardo, the two most important requisites for painting were a knowledge of perspective and of anatomy. "Masaccio," Leonardo wrote in his *Treatise on Painting,* "showed by the perfection of his work how those who took as their standard anything other than nature, the supreme guide of all the masters, were wearying themselves in vain." Leon Battista Alberti, the architect, humanist, and spokesman for the early pioneers of the Renaissance, laid the groundwork for Leonardo's theoretical writings on art in his treatises on sculpture and painting, written between 1430 and 1435. By this time the spirit of discovery of early-fifteenth-century Florentine art had begun to subside. Different values — pietism, decorative refinement, sophisticated visual effects — dominated the art of the middle of the century. In Leonardo the spirit of the early pioneers came to life once more. He went back to the heart and core of the new art, and thus laid the foundation for its greatest flowering in the classic style of the High Renaissance.

Leonardo's personality, like the regions that he probed in his art, is mysterious and obscure. His *Notebooks,* into which he poured his observations and thoughts for over thirty years, contain not a single reference to his personal feelings. It is not surprising that the veil behind which his personality is hidden should have given rise to a "Romance of Leonardo," the most famous example of which is Freud's essay, written in 1910, on Leonardo's memory of a childhood dream, which was the only allusion in the *Notebooks* to the artist's youth.

He was born at Anchiano, near Vinci — not far from Florence — on April 15, 1452. His father was the notary Ser Piero da Vinci, and his mother was a peasant woman called Caterina. Leonardo was brought up on his father's farm until he was fifteen, "watching," as Walter Pater said, "the lizards and glow worms and other strange creatures which haunt an Italian vineyard." His absorbed interest in organic life surely goes back to this period of his boyhood, spent far from the urban, literary milieu of Medicean Florence. Although his father lived mainly in Florence, Leonardo himself did not move to the city until 1469 when, at the unusually late age of 17, he was apprenticed to the painter-sculptor Andrea del Verrocchio, then engaged in the making of the ornate bronze tomb of Piero de' Medici in Brunelleschi's Old Sacristy of the Medicean church of San Lorenzo. In 1472 Leonardo was enrolled in the painters' guild, but he remained the collaborator of Verrocchio and continued to live in his house until 1476. In January, 1478, he received a commission from the commune of Florence. It can be assumed that by then he must have been established as an independent master.

Of Leonardo's appearance, Vasari tells us that "his personal beauty could not be exaggerated, and his every movement was grace itself." He lived in a private world of strange interests and images. Having agreed to paint a shield for one of his father's peasants, "he resolved to do the Medusa head to terrify all beholders," Vasari relates. "To a room, to which he alone had access, Leonardo took lizards, newts, maggots, snakes, butterflies, locusts, bats, and other animals of the kind, out of which he composed a horrible and terrible monster." When his father saw the work, "Ser Piero, taken unaware, started back, not thinking . . . that the face which he saw was painted, and was beating a retreat when Leonardo detained him and said, 'this work has served its purpose; take it away, then, as it has produced the effect intended.' "

This shield has not come down to us, though we know from Vasari that "in a short time it came into the hands of the Duke of Milan." But the story is more than an anecdote about a young artist's prank. The implication that once a work had "produced the effect intended" Leonardo would lose interest in it provides a valuable insight into his habit of leaving paintings unfinished. If what matters is the effect, then as long as it is achieved it is relatively unimportant whether a picture is finished or not. We know that Michelangelo would leave sculptures in marble unfinished when he felt that to continue working on them would have diminished their expressive effect. But Leonardo was the originator of the concept that in art the effect justifies the means, thereby enabling artists to liberate themselves from the exacting standards of performance laid down by the craft guilds. Artists came to be thought of as men of ideas rather than as craftsmen, and it was with approbation rather than censure that Vasari wrote of Leonardo that "he felt that his hand would be unable to realize the perfect creations of his imagination."

The year Leonardo entered the shop of Verrocchio, Piero de' Medici, ruler of Florence for five years, died, and was succeeded by his son Lorenzo the Magnificent. A year earlier Piero had organized a tournament in honor of the Florentine beauty Lucrezia Doni, for which the city's greatest artists, including Botticelli, the brothers Antonio and Piero Pollaiuolo, and Verrocchio, had supplied decorations. They were employed again for the pageant celebrating Lorenzo's marriage to the Roman heiress Clarice Orsini on June 4, 1469, and for the climax of these spectacles, the tournament given by Lorenzo's younger brother Giuliano in 1475. Three years later Giuliano was dead, the victim of a conspiracy to overthrow the Medici led by the Pazzi family and abetted by Pope Sixtus IV. The attempted coup failed, but it precipitated a war between Florence and an alliance of Italian states headed by the Pope. Florence was saved only by the diplomatic genius of Lorenzo.

It is one of the ironies of history that this most cultivated patron of his day took virtually no notice of Leonardo. But the indifference was mutual. Leonardo, with his scientific and mathematical bent, was not in the least interested in the Platonically-oriented intellectual world of the Magnificent. While he was with Verrocchio, Vasari tells us, Leonardo "not only practiced his profession, but all those in which design has a part. Possessed of a divine and marvellous intellect, and being an excellent geometrician, he not only worked in sculpture . . . but also prepared many architectural plans and elevations, and he was the first to propose canalizing the Arno from Pisa to Florence. He made designs for . . . engines to go by water, and as painting was to be his profession he studied drawing from life. He made models and designs . . . by means of levers, cranes and winches to raise and draw heavy weights; he devised a method for cleansing ports, and to raise water from great depths, schemes which his brain never ceased to evolve." Clearly he was not the man to satisfy the allegorical and literary requirements of Florentine patrons of the 1470s. When in 1482 an opportunity presented itself for him to go to Milan he immediately seized it, and there found a congenial and appreciative patron in Duke Ludovico Sforza. Leonardo remained in Milan until the city fell to the French in 1499.

From the point of view of artistic production the decade before Leonardo's departure was one of the richest of his career. His earliest dated work is a pen drawing of a *Landscape,* inscribed "August 5, 1473" (Figure 2). It is a brilliant example of the shorthand which Leonardo invented for rendering in terms of light and shade the rhythmic movements of nature — of the formation of cliffs, of foliage, and of the flow of water. By means of it he was able to express the truth that all things are seen in an atmosphere of light and air, and to represent nature as an animate, living being. In a drawing of *The Deluge* done more than forty years later (Figure 20), he formulated such an image of nature — a visual expression of the Renaissance doctrine of pantheism — in terms of the cosmic energy of whirling spirals of water. No juxtaposition could show more clearly the unity of Leonardo's evolution than a comparison between these two drawings. The youthful empirical observer became, as an old man, a visionary. Yet his belief in life as flux — a belief anticipating by four centuries Henri Bergson's theory of the *élan vital* — remained the same.

Several paintings from the period of Leonardo's collaboration with Verrocchio have come down to us, though opinion is divided both on their dates and on the extent of Leonardo's participation in their execution. The *Annunciation* in the Uffizi (Slides 3 and 4) and the *Madonna with the Vase* (Slide 5) were probably painted between 1473 and 1475, the same period in which Leonardo added the angel and the distant landscape — reminiscent of the *Landscape* of 1473 — in the *Baptism of Christ* by Verrocchio (Slides 1 and 2). A small panel of the *Annunciation* in the Louvre (part of the predella of an altarpiece in the cathedral of Pistoia designed by Verrocchio and executed for the most part by his pupil Lorenzo di Credi) is a more harmonious work than the Uffizi *Annunciation,* and if not painted by the young Leonardo himself reflects what must have been the organic unity and expressiveness of his earliest style in painting more perfectly than any other known work. At about the time he set up his studio Leonardo painted the ravishing portrait of *Ginevra de' Benci* (Slide 6), an exquisite precursor of the *Mona Lisa* (Slide 17), sur-

Figure 2.
Landscape (1473)
pen, 7½″ x 11¼″
Uffizi, Florence

passing the later work in delicacy of tone and modeling. The *Benois Madonna* (Figure 3), begun by Leonardo in 1470/80 and continued with the assistance of a pupil in 1500, is the first of his compositions in which one can clearly feel the rhythmic structure of the High Renaissance style. Similarly stately, contained gestures are put into play in the unfinished *St. Jerome* of about 1480 (Slide 7), though with strained, expressionistic overtones. The first triumph of the emerging style and the first comprehensive demonstration of its potentialities is the *Adoration of the Magi,* begun in 1481 and left unfinished when Leonardo went to Milan (Slides 8 and 9).

Each of Leonardo's paintings was preceded by studies in the form of drawings, in which he tried out different possibilities and gradually worked his way toward a final solution. Some of these, like the brilliant *Study for the Benois Madonna* (Figure 4), are spontaneously done sketches in which the forms seem to be plucked out of the air as they are rapidly noted down. Others, such as the *Study for the Adoration of the Magi* (Figure 5), are detailed working drawings. In an earlier sketch for the *Adoration* the staircases and the riders in the background were seen through an open shed with a gabled roof. This later sketch with its carefully drawn perspective study of the background shows Leonardo still thinking in terms of framing it with an architectural enclosure. In the painting (Slide 8) he abandoned this device and substituted for it the more ingenious compositional stratagem of the two trees just to the right of center. But he represented the arches and staircases — an imaginary ruin of a Roman stadium — almost exactly as he had worked them out in the drawing.

"There are three branches of perspective," Leonardo wrote in his *Treatise on Painting.* "The first deals with the reasons for the apparent diminution of objects as they recede from the eye. The second contains the way in which colors vary as they recede from the eye. The third and last is concerned with the explanation of how objects in a picture ought to be less finished proportionately to their remoteness. The names are as follows: linear perspective, the perspective of color, the perspective of disappearance." *The Study for the Adoration* is obviously most concerned with the first of these. It is the most detailed fifteenth-century preparatory drawing of a linear perspective construction that has come down to us. Yet like the *Landscape* of 1473 it is alive with the play of light and shadow and with atmosphere, and vividly suggests the other two modes of perspective (which are both usually designated by the term "aerial perspective") as well. Leonardo may have thought of this drawing as a picture in its own right, for it is executed on specially prepared pink paper — a practice he recommends in his *Treatise on Painting* — first in silverpoint and then, to give it body, with pen and wash.

Leonardo went to Milan for any one, or all, of three reasons. Vasari says that he was invited "with great ceremony by the duke to play the lyre, in which that prince greatly delighted. Leonardo took his own instrument, made by himself in silver, and shaped like a horse's head, a curious and novel idea to render the harmonies more loud and sonorous, so that he surpassed all the musicians who had assembled there." Although it would not have

Figure 3.
Benois Madonna (about 1478–1480)
transferred from wood to canvas
18⅞″ x 12⅜″
Hermitage, Leningrad

Figure 4.
Study for the Benois Madonna
(sometimes known as
Madonna with the Fruit Plate)
(about 1478–1480)
silverpoint, pen, and wash
12⅞″ x 9¾″
Louvre, Paris

Figure 5.
*Study for the Adoration
of the Magi* (1481–1482)
silverpoint, pen, and wash
6½″ x 11⅜″
Uffizi, Florence

been surprising for Leonardo to go to Milan as a musician to entertain the court rather than as a painter, the Duke may also have summoned him for more practical reasons. Sometime in 1482 Leonardo had sent to him a petition for employment, chiefly as a military engineer, and the real reason for his going may have been that he was needed in this capacity. Of the ten services he offered the Duke in his petition, nine were inventions of "instruments of war," both offensive and defensive, such as bridges, armored cars, cannon, and even, "if it should happen that the engagement is at sea, plans for constructing many engines most suitable either for attack or defense, and ships which can resist the fire of all the heaviest cannon, and powder and smoke." Only the tenth service does not concern war. "In times of peace," Leonardo writes, "I believe that I can give you as complete satisfaction as anyone else in architecture in the construction of buildings both public and private, and in conducting water from one place to another." Almost as an afterthought, he adds that "also I can execute sculpture in marble, bronze, or clay and also painting, in which my work will stand comparison with that of anyone else. Moreover, I would undertake the work of the bronze

13

horse, which shall perpetuate with immortal glory and eternal honor the auspicious memory of the Prince your father and of the illustrious house of Sforza." Leonardo is here referring to the equestrian monument of Francesco Sforza, the first of his family to rule Milan, who had died in 1465. The monument had been proposed by his son Galeazzo Maria as early as 1473. But when Ludovico made himself master of Milan in 1481, five years after Galeazzo Maria's assassination, nothing further had been done. Bound by family honor to pursue the project, however, the new Duke finally entrusted the execution of the monument to Leonardo in 1483. Perhaps it was this that he had in mind when he summoned Leonardo.

We know that Leonardo worked on the "bronze horse" for sixteen years. It was never cast. When a model had finally been approved ten years after Leonardo had begun, the metal that had been set aside for it had to be used instead for casting cannon. Leonardo's first conception of the statue, a rearing horse, its front legs poised over a fallen enemy, is preserved in a beautiful silverpoint drawing of about 1485 showing Francesco Sforza as a general leading his troops in battle (Figure 6). In 1489 this design had to be abandoned as technically impractical. But on April 23, 1490, Leonardo made a note that "I began the horse again." A life-size clay model of this second project, with the horse in the traditional

Figure 6.
Study for the Sforza Monument
(about 1485), silverpoint
5⅞" x 7¼"
Royal Library, Windsor Castle

walking pose, was exhibited in 1493 at the wedding of the Emperor Maximilian and Bianca Maria Sforza, the daughter of Galeazzo Maria. Thereafter it was placed in the citadel, where Leonardo continued to work on it. When the French entered Milan in October, 1499, they used it for target practice. In the end the model was moved to Ferrara, where it fell apart.

Under Ludovico, called *"Il Moro"* because of his dark complexion, Milan was the richest city in Europe. Its court was said to have been "the most brilliant in all Europe since the Burgundian court had ceased to exist." Leonardo played a part in every phase of its modernization and embellishment. He worked as a city planner, architect, designer of court festivals, and as a structural, military, and hydraulic engineer, all in addition to his activity in sculpture and in what Vasari called his "profession" — painting. But our knowledge of what he did comes almost entirely from documents and drawings. A typical example of one of his many projects that were never carried out is an intricate design for the corner towers of the ducal palace, the Castello Sforzesco, on the same sheet as a study for the head of St. James the Elder in *The Last Supper* (Figure 7; for the head in the fresco see Slides 14 and 16).

Figure 7.
Study for the Apostle James the Elder in The Last Supper (about 1495), red chalk and pen 9⅞″ x 6¾″. Royal Library, Windsor Castle

Isabella d'Este, Marchesa of Mantua, wrote of Milan and Leonardo, "This is the school of the master and of those who know, the home of art and understanding." The Marchesa was a great connoisseur of painting, and what she had in mind were the pictures by Leonardo and his pupils which adorned the palaces and churches of the city — the "New Athens," as Milan styled itself. Only five paintings by Leonardo himself have survived from the period of seventeen years he spent there. They are *The Madonna of the Rocks* (Slides 10 and 11), painted between 1483 and 1486; the portraits of *Cecilia Gallerani* (Slide 12) and of a *Musician* (Slide 13), both of about 1485; *The Last Supper* (Slides 14 to 16), begun in 1495 and finished in 1498; and a room with ornamental frescoes of interlaced branches and leaves in the Castello Sforzesco, the *Sala delle Asse,* which he painted in 1498.

The intellectual atmosphere of the Milanese court was very different from that of the palace and the villas of Lorenzo de' Medici. In Florence the great men were philosophers and poets, such as Pico della Mirandola and Poliziano. In Milan they were Galeazzo Sanseverino, the general and strategist of Ludovico's armies; Donato Bramante, the architect; Luca Pacioli, the mathematician and, of course, Leonardo da Vinci, the "master of those who know," as Dante described Aristotle in the *Divine Comedy.* He could supply Sanseverino with ideas for "an infinite number of different engines of attack and defense," as he had written in his petition of Ludovico *il Moro.* He designed the illustrations for Luca Pacioli's book *Divine Proportion,* published in Venice in 1509. And he had a decisive influence on Bramante, who derived his interest in centrally planned churches from the designs for centralized buildings which fill the pages of Leonardo's *Notebooks* in the years around 1490. The upper half of one of these pages (Figure 8) shows a building which, except in its proportions and in the form of its dome, contains all the essential elements of Bramante's plan of 1505 for the rebuilding of the great basilica of St. Peter's in Rome.

Unlike the architectural drawing accompanying the study for the head of St. James (Figure 7), Leonardo's designs for centralized churches were not studies for actual buildings. They were part of a projected *Treatise on Architecture* in which he planned to assemble all the notes and sketches on architectural matters that he had begun to make shortly after his arrival in Milan. It was at this time that he also began his first systematic studies in anatomy, biology, mathematics, physics, and mechanics. He outlined treatises on *Anatomy* and *Mechanics,* subjects which he pursued with increasing absorption for the rest of his life, and made the majority of the notes which after his death were put together as the *Treatise on Painting.* One of the fields of mechanics which intrigued Leonardo the most was flight. Between 1503 and 1506, when he was once more in Florence, he wrote a treatise *On the Flight of Birds,* a work of fundamental importance for the science of aerology. But in Milan he concentrated on experiments with human flight. "A bird is an instrument working according to mathematical law," he wrote, "which . . . is within the

Figure 8.
Designs for a Centralized Building (about 1490), pen, 9¼" x 6¾"
Institut de France, Paris

capacity of man to reproduce . . . ." One of his early designs for a flying machine (Figure 9) had a wooden framework and two movable wings which were operated by pulleys connected to the flyer's feet and by a manually worked windlass.

Painting, as defined in Leonardo's treatise on it, "is the grandchild of nature; for all visible things derive their existence from nature, and from these same things is born painting. So therefore we may justly speak of it as the grandchild of nature and as related to God Himself." The painter, Leonardo says, must be universal, "since we know that painting embraces and includes in itself every object produced by nature or resulting from the fortuitous action of men, in short, all that the eye can see . . . ." Painting must be based on mathematics, for it depends "on the harmonious proportioning of the parts that make up the whole"; and proportions, as the Renaissance understood them, were a visualization of mathematical laws. Perspective, Leonardo's first requirement for painting, is the mathematical proportioning of space. The classical canon of proportions for the human figure provides a system of mathematical relationships for intelligibly representing the anatomical structure of the body. Leonardo's famous illustration of this canon is based on a passage in the *Ten Books of Architecture* by the first-century B.C. Roman architect Vitruvius (Figure 10). The human body according to Vitruvius, can be circumscribed by both a circle and a square. "If you set your legs so far apart as to take a fourteenth part from your height," Leonardo wrote in explanation of the drawing, "and you open and raise your arms until you touch the line of the crown of the head with your middle fingers, you must know that the center of the circle formed by the extremities of the outstretched limbs will be the navel, and the space between the legs will form an equilateral triangle." When the body is inscribed in the square, resulting from the fact that "the span of a man's outstretched arms is equal to his height," its fulcrum is displaced from the navel to the *os sacrum.*

On October 5, 1499, a French army under Louis XII entered Milan. Ludovico, after having attempted to reconquer the city, was taken prisoner. His one request during his captivity, for a copy of Dante's *Divine Comedy,* was refused. He died in the dungeon of the royal castle at Loches in 1508. With the fall of his patron Leonardo left Milan to look for employment elsewhere. Together with Luca Pacioli he set off in December, 1499, going first to the court of his admirer Isabella d'Este at Mantua, and then to Venice, where he drew up plans for fortifications to secure the republic against naval attacks by the Turks. In April, 1500, he returned to Florence, after an absence of almost eighteen years.

Within a few weeks he was at work on a cartoon for a *St. Anne, Virgin and Child* which, Vasari writes, "not only filled every artist with wonder, but, when it was finished and set up in the room, men and women, young and old, flocked to see it for two days, as if it were a festival, and all marvelled at its excellence. The face of the Virgin displays all the simplicity and beauty which can shed grace on the Mother of God, showing the modesty and humility of a Virgin contentedly happy, in seeing the beauty of her Son,

Figure 9.
Design of a Flying Machine
(about 1490–1495)
chalk and pen
10¼″ x 7⅜″
Biblioteca Ambrosiana, Milan

18

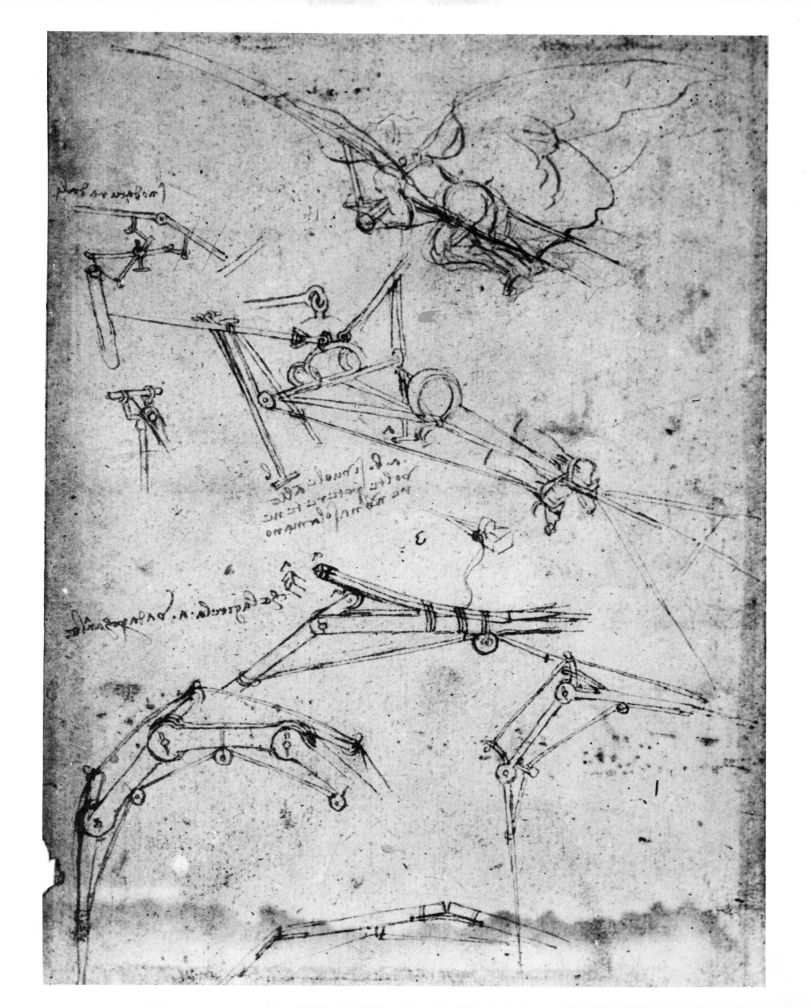

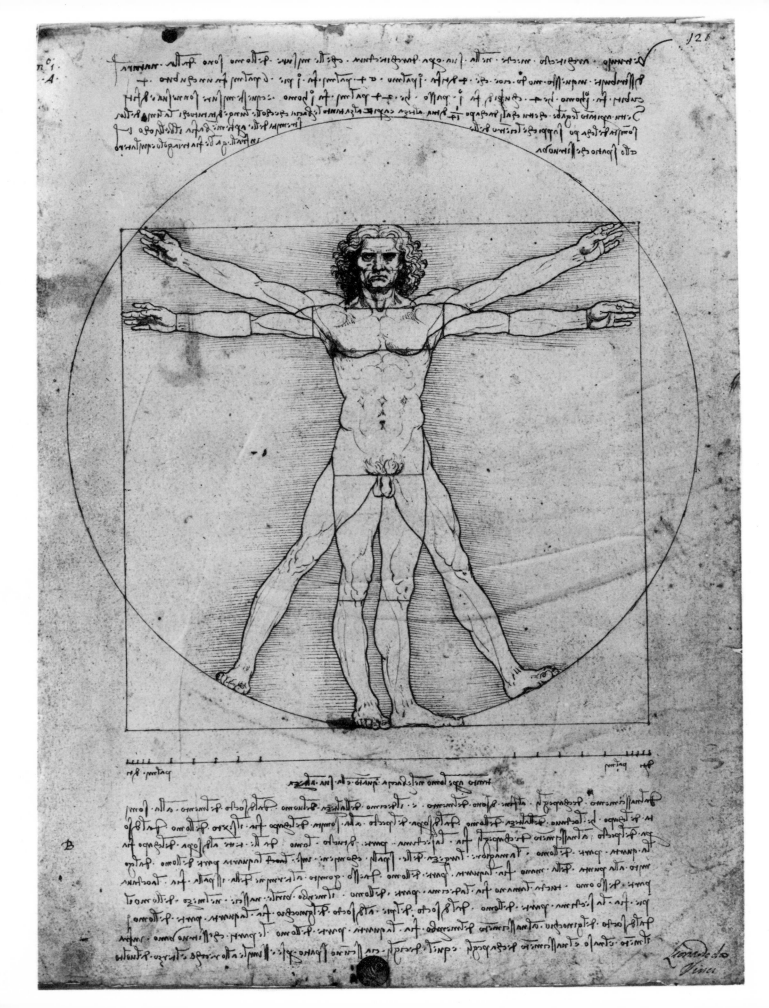

whom she tenderly holds in her lap. As she regards Him the little St. John at her feet is caressing a lamb, while St. Anne smiles in her great joy at seeing her earthly progeny become divine, a conception worthy of the great intellect and genius of Leonardo." This cartoon was sent to France and has been lost, but on the basis of a detailed description by Fra Pietro da Novellara, an agent of Isabella d'Este who was unsuccessfully trying to persuade Leonardo to work for the Marchesa, its composition has been recognized in a replica by Brescianino now in Berlin. The lost cartoon was Leonardo's second design for a group of St. Anne, Mary, and Christ. The first was a cartoon made in Milan between the completion of *The Last Supper* and the fall of the city to the French (Figure 11). And the third was a painting done during Leonardo's second Milanese period (Slides 18 and 19), which in certain respects corresponds rather closely to Vasari's description of the lost cartoon.

Three phases can be discerned in Leonardo's development as a painter: an early one, through the *Adoration of the Magi;* the phase of his mature style, from *The Madonna of the Rocks* to *The Last Supper;* and a late phase, beginning with the first cartoon of the *St. Anne, Virgin and Child.* This late style is characterized by the monumentality of figures, whose sculptural presence fills the whole of the picture, the suppression of naturalism in favor of idealization, and a broad, tonal definition of three-dimensional form. The figures of the first cartoon (Figure 11), in their grace and their majesty, are truly comparable, as Bernard Berenson recognized, to the seated figures on the pediment of the Parthenon.

From May, 1502, until March of the following year Leonardo was employed as an inspector of fortifications and military engineer for Cesare Borgia, then the general of the armies under the command of Pope Alexander VI. He drew maps and plans of cities, which, beyond their immediate usefulness, were to be important stepping stones in the development of modern cartography. On his return to Florence Leonardo received a commission from the commune of Florence to paint a mural on a subject from Florentine history on one wall of the council chamber of the city hall, the Palazzo della Signoria. The other wall was assigned to Michelangelo, whose fresco, like Leonardo's, has survived only in copies. Leonardo chose as his theme the fight for the enemy standard at the battle of Anghiari, an engagement fought on June 29, 1441, some thirty miles to the southeast of Florence. In this battle Florentine arms won a decisive victory over Milanese forces under the command of Niccolo Piccinino, thus bringing to an end the threat of a Milanese invasion of Tuscany. Leonardo worked on the cartoon for this mural, which has been lost, from October, 1503, until February, 1505. The fate of the fresco itself is described by Vasari: "Thinking that he [Leonardo] could paint on the wall in oils, he made a composition so thick for laying on the wall that when he continued his painting it began to run and spoil what had been begun, so that in a short time he was forced to abandon it." The unfinished and deteriorating fresco was covered over when the council chamber was redecorated with frescoes by Vasari in 1565.

Several copies of Leonardo's composition had been made and preserved in engravings.

Figure 10.
Illustration of the Proportions of the Human Figure (after Vitruvius about 1485–1490) 13½" x 8¾" Galleria dell'Accademia, Venice

21

From one of these Rubens drew the magnificent sketch of the central group (Figure 12) which, judging from Leonardo's many studies, conveys better than any other known version the spirit of the original. In working out the composition of the central group Leonardo had come to concentrate on the expression of unbridled rage gripping both horses and men. The centripetal forces of the group, as if their fury had for a split second attained a state of equilibrium, are for this moment held in poised, motionless balance.

Leonardo made innumerable studies for the *Battle of Anghiari,* especially of the heads of the figures and of horses. One idea above all seems to have intrigued him: the rage binding horses and men together. In a splendid study of horses and horses' heads (Figure 13) there are, in the lower part of the sheet to the left of center, the rapidly drawn heads of a lion and a man, both charged with the same "leonine" expression of fury, similar to that of the horses' heads surrounding them. The outcome of such a study was the more finished drawing of the head of a warrior (Figure 14), which preserves all of the wild animal fierceness of the heads in the earlier sketch.

Figure 12.
Peter Paul Rubens,
copy of the *Battle of Anghiari*
(about 1615)
chalk, pen, and gouache
17¾″ x 25¼″
Louvre, Paris

Figure 11.
Cartoon for St. Anne,
Virgin and Child
(1498–1499)
charcoal heightened with white
54⅞″ x 39⅞″
National Gallery, London

Figure 14.
Study for the Battle of Anghiari
(1503–1504)
black and red chalk
7½″ x 7⅜″
Museum of Fine Arts, Budapest

Figure 13.
Study for the Battle of Anghiari
(1503–1504)
pen, 7¾″ x 12⅛″
Royal Library, Windsor Castle

During the years in which he worked on the mural Leonardo also painted the portrait of *Mona Lisa* (Slide 17) and a picture of *Leda,* which in the course of the sixteenth century was taken to France and later supposedly burned. It is known through several copies and a number of drawings, the most evolved of which is the beautiful small sketch in Rotterdam (Figure 15). The legend of Leda is the most sensuous of all Greek myths. She was embraced by Zeus in the guise of a swan and from their union brought forth two eggs; from one egg was born Helen and from the other Castor and Pollux. The full-bodied, undulating figure in Leonardo's drawing — the prototype of the classic *contrapposto* of the female nude in the art of the High Renaissance and Mannerism — is a metaphorical embodiment of the female principle of creation. Its motion is echoed by the spiraling blades of grass at the bottom of the drawing, as it is in the *Study of a "Star of Bethlehem"* of about the same time (Figure 16). The spiral became for Leonardo the symbol of the life cycle in nature — the rhythmic alternation and recurrence of creation and destruction. His matchless skill as an artist — in perspective, chiaroscuro, and proportions — is put to the service of formulating an image of the "Star of Bethlehem" not only as a living, growing plant but also as a symbol of the eternal flux of nature.

Figure 15.
[lower left] *Kneeling Leda*
(about 1506)
black chalk and pen
4⅞″ x 4⅜″
Van Beuningen-Boymans Museum
Rotterdam

Figure 16.
[lower right]
Study of a "Star of Bethlehem"
(about 1505–1506)
red chalk and pen
7¾″ x 6¼″
Royal Library, Windsor Castle

In 1506 Leonardo interrupted his work on the *Battle of Anghiari* and, released from his contractual obligations by the Florentine Signoria, moved once more to Milan, this time at the invitation of the French king. With the exception of a visit to Florence from September, 1506, to July, 1507, to help the sculptor Gianfrancesco Rustici with the bronze group of *St. John the Baptist Preaching,* now above the north door of the Florentine Baptistry, he remained in Milan until 1513. During these years he once more took up the project, outlined twenty years earlier, of a *Treatise on Anatomy* and concentrated on it all the artistic powers at his command. The anatomical drawings of this period (Figure 17) are even more astonishing for the clarity with which they show the complex construction of the body than for their accuracy. They became models for all future scientific illustrations. But they are also more than that. "An artist," it has been said, "is a man who seeks new structures in which to order and simplify his sense of the reality of life." Seen from this point of view, Leonardo's late anatomical drawings are not only superb illustrations, but also remarkable works of art.

In his other scientific studies during the second Milanese period he turned aside from engineering and mechanics toward the investigation of inorganic nature — especially the formation of the earth and the phenomena of air and water — and the attempt to formulate a comprehensive cosmology. Reflections of these preoccupations are found in the distant landscape of the painting of *St. Anne, Virgin and Child,* which was completed about 1510 (Slide 18).

Charles d'Amboise died on March 10, 1511, whereupon the governorship of Milan was divided between two generals. The first, Gaston de Foix, lost his life in the following year after gaining the victory at the battle of Ravenna. The other was Gian Giacomo Trivulzio (in earlier days a bitter rival of Ludovico *il Moro*), for whom Leonardo began the design of an equestrian monument. Although it was never erected, Leonardo did many studies for both the statue and the base on which it was to be placed. Some show the horse in a walking pose. In others the horse, as in the first project for the Sforza monument (Figure 6), is rearing over a vanquished foe (Figure 18). This particular study is a good example of Leonardo's late drawing style. The hatching curves inward with the form and thus emphasizes its sculptural quality, rather than moving across it so as to bring out the play of light and shadow, as we find it in Leonardo's earlier drawings.

Some time after the change of governors — though Milan remained in the hands of the French — Leonardo made the designs for a court masquerade, of which several costume studies have been preserved (Figure 19). The high point of such festivals usually was a play, in which the visual effect of the staging and the décor was considered far more important than the text. Leonardo had already designed such theatrical productions during his first Milanese period. For the marriage of Giangaleazzo Sforza, the son of Galeazzo Maria, to Isabella of Aragon on January 13, 1490, he had put on *A Festival in Paradise,* which included movable mountains that could open and close; and in 1496 he had directed a play called *Jupiter and Danae* in the palace of Gianfrancesco Sanseverino, the

26

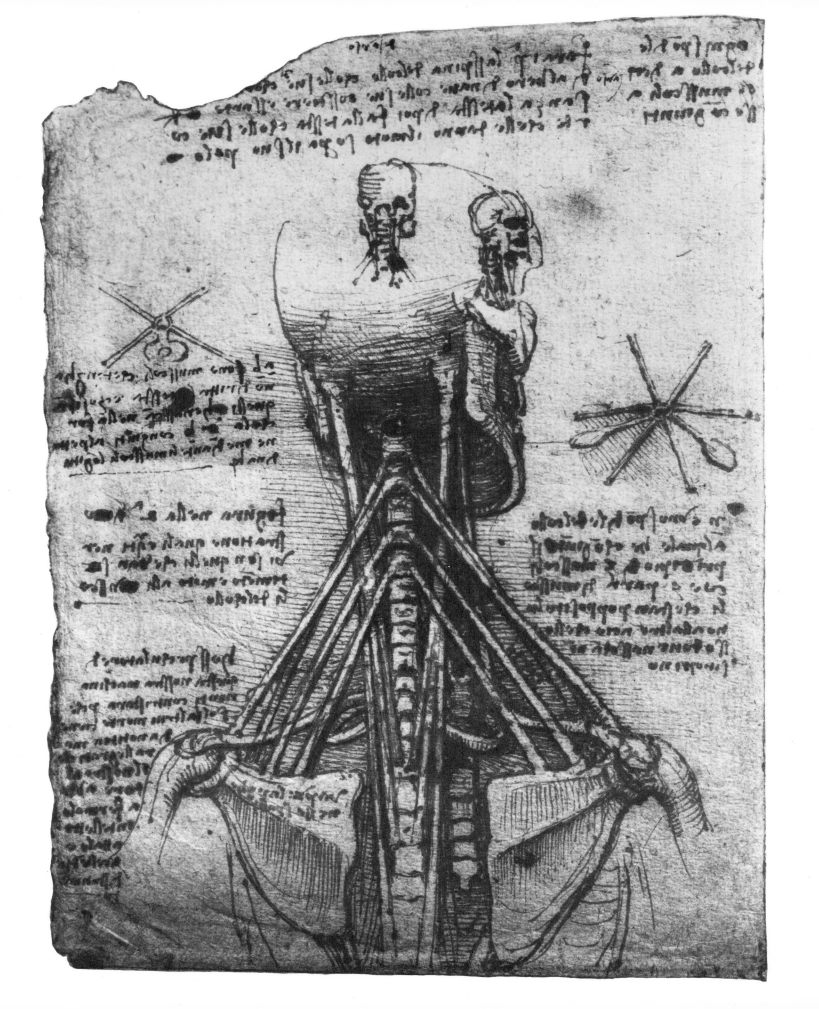

Figure 18.
Studies for the Trivulzio Monument
(about 1511–1512)
pen, 11″ x 7¾″
Royal Library, Windsor Castle

Figure 19.
Costume Study
(about 1512)
black chalk, pen, and wash
about 7½″ x 5″
Royal Library, Windsor Castle

brother of Ludovico's general. After the fall of Ludovico the Milanese court had come to reflect the fashion and the tastes of its French masters. The romantic air and quality of artifice in Leonardo's costume studies of that time suggest something of this French spirit. These studies cannot be very different from the lost designs that he did in France for a festival given by Francis I in 1517 at Argenten.

In May, 1513, Giovanni de' Medici, the second son of Lorenzo the Magnificent, was elected to the throne of St. Peter as Pope Leo X. On September 24 of that year Leonardo, drawn to Rome by the new Pope's liberality to artists, left Milan for the Eternal City. After stopping in Florence, he arrived in Rome in December and was given lodgings in the Belvedere of the Vatican. Leo lived and ruled according to the dictum attributed to him on the day of his election: "Now that God has given us the papacy, let us enjoy it!" The greatest artists of Italy, men younger and more worldly than Leonardo, were congregating at the papal court in Rome. Raphael was working on the frescoes in the Pope's apartments — the so-called *stanze* — where he had already completed the *School of Athens*. And Michelangelo had finished the decoration of the Sistine ceiling. Leonardo, at the age of sixty-one, was an old man, melancholy, withdrawn, no longer interested in anything beyond his own dreams and intuitions. In his *Self-Portrait* (Figure 1) of about this time he looks rather like the aged Tolstoi. He devoted himself almost exclusively to his scientific studies, though the Pope, in consequence of an intrigue instigated by a German maker of mirrors, a man known as Giovanni degli Specchi, forbade him to continue his work in anatomy. One of the few records of what he did in Rome is a passage in his *Notebooks* to the effect that "on the 7th day of July, at the 23rd hour" — the year is not given — he finished a treatise on geometrical games, *De Ludo Geometrico*. In the thirty-nine months he stayed at the Vatican Leonardo did only one painting, the *St. John the Baptist* in the Louvre (Slide 20).

On the reverse of a paper showing the head of a bearded old man, he made studies of spiraling eddies of water, and a note comparing their motion to that of locks of hair. Here, and in a number of similar drawings, his fascination with the movement of water and with the shape of the spiral reach their culmination (Figure 20). The swirling cascades of water represent the principle of life in nature in terms of a cosmic energy whose creative and destructive power consumes the earth itself. These apocalyptic visions of the end of the world are closely related to Leonardo's descriptions, added to the *Treatise on Painting* while he was in Rome, of how to represent the Deluge: "You should show how fragments of mountains, which have already been stripped bare by the rushing torrents, fall headlong into these very torrents and choke up the valleys, until the pent-up rivers rise in flood and cover the wide plain or their inhabitants," he says in one passage of this long, detailed account. Elsewhere in it we read that "the swollen waters will sweep around the pool which contains them, striking in eddying whirlpools against the different obstacles, and leaping into the air in muddy foam; then falling back, the beaten water will again be

Figure 20.
The Deluge (about 1515–1517)
black chalk, 6¼″ x 8¼″
Royal Library, Windsor Castle

dashed into the air." The drawings of *The Deluge* are Leonardo's testament. Their harmonious, spiraling, self-generating and self-annihilating rhythms are the ultimate metaphor for Leonardo's intuition of a cosmic order, an order embodied in the principle of flux.

In January, 1517, Leonardo left Rome with his devoted assistant, Francesco Melzi, to go to France at the invitation of Francis I, the twenty-three-year-old king who had succeeded Louis XII to the throne in 1515. Leonardo lived in a manor house, Cloux, near the royal residence at Amboise. He was given the title of "First Painter, Architect, and Engineer to the King." But his powers were beginning to fail. His only recorded activity in France are designs for a palace and gardens for the king's mother at Romorantin. Benvenuto Cellini, in his *Autobiography,* reported that in 1536 he heard Francis I say "that he did believe no other man had been born who knew as much as Leonardo in sculpture, painting, and architecture, so that he was a very great philosopher." Leonardo died at Cloux on May 2, 1519, leaving to the devoted Melzi his drawings and manuscripts.

A recent book of reproductions of the work of the American photographer Walker Evans has as its motto Matisse's dictum, *"L'exactitude n'est pas la verité."* Exactness is not the truth. Both this motto and the book itself are examples, chosen at random, of how much we owe to Leonardo da Vinci. Having carried the empirical study of nature further than any other man of his generation, he acknowledged at the end of his life that the truth is not synonymous with the data of exact observation, but lies behind them. And the fact that we look at photographs at all — that we consider pictures made by the single eye of the camera a meaningful and indispensable means of communication—is an outgrowth of Leonardo's belief that the key to knowledge and wisdom is in the eye. What we see and what we think we see are in large measure consequences of his achievements.

COMMENTARY ON THE SLIDES

COMMENTARY ON THE SLIDES

1: THE BAPTISM OF CHRIST by Andrea del Verrocchio (about 1473–1475)
wood, 69⅞″ x 59⅝″, Uffizi, Florence

Andrea del Verrocchio was the last of the great Florentine all-around artist-craftsmen of the fifteenth century. He was mainly a sculptor; but he was able to carry out commissions in any kind of material — precious stones, gold, copper, iron, ivory, alabaster, and, of course, painting. As the master of both Leonardo da Vinci and Perugino (through whom his influence was transmitted to the young Raphael) he was the seminal figure in the transition from the style of the fifteenth century to that of the High Renaissance. But, like Michelangelo, he was not a born painter. One has to look at his sculpture to see the poetic intuitions and the imaginative power of which he was capable.

The Baptism of Christ is the most important and characteristic of the small number of Verrocchio's paintings. Its style is hard and linear. Each form is rendered with such clarity and force that they compete for attention rather than being subordinated to a harmonizing design. The two protagonists express what is most noble in fifteenth-century Florentine art: dignity and manliness. There is nothing elegant about them. Their severity is unrelieved by the *sfumato* — the blurring of contours — intimated in the angel at the far left, which was painted by the young Leonardo da Vinci.

Verrocchio's line does not sing, like Botticelli's, nor does it have the mobility of the line of Antonio Pollaiuolo. It is, like Andrea del Castagno's, firm and tense, bounding figures whose form and human fibre are indomitably tough. The heroic stuff of which they are made no doubt provides the vital clue to the great importance of Verrocchio for the future of Renaissance art.

2: THE BAPTISM OF CHRIST (detail)
by Andrea del Verrocchio and Leonardo da Vinci

Leonardo's angel in *The Baptism of Christ* was mentioned for the first time in a description of Florence of 1510 and later by Vasari, who says that when Leonardo was first apprenticed to Verrocchio, "his master happened to be painting a picture of St. John baptizing Christ. For this the young Leonardo did an angel holding some clothes, and, although quite young, he made it far better than the figures of Andrea. The latter would afterwards never touch colors, chagrined that a child should know more than he."

Whatever the reason for the decline of Verrocchio's activity as a painter, it is undeniable that Leonardo's angel went far beyond what Verrocchio could have done or conceived. Verrocchio's angel has the fixed, unseeing gaze of a graven image, whereas the angel by Leonardo looks up at Christ and St. John with an expression of empathy and comprehension. Leonardo has given him the mobility and warmth of life — not life as we ordinarily know it, however, but in a form of ideal physical and spiritual beauty. Such is the gentleness of the contours and tonal transitions in the angel's face, the grace with which he turns his head, and the delicacy of his spiraling cascade of hair, that he seems to be not only alive but truly divine.

His finely rendered drapery is related to a number of drapery studies with similarly crisp, peaked folds which Leonardo did at this time. According to Vasari, Leonardo "often made figures in clay which he covered with a soft linen dipped in clay, and then set himself to draw them with great patience on a particular kind of Reims cloth or prepared linen; and he executed some of them in black and white with the point of the brush to a marvel." The drapery of the angel must have been painted by the same method and shows the same careful observation of light and texture as the studies mentioned by Vasari.

3: THE ANNUNCIATION (about 1473–1475), wood, 35⅝" x 85¾", Uffizi, Florence

The Uffizi *Annunciation* was originally in the Convent of Monte Oliveto, just beyond the walls of Florence to the southwest. It is an example of very high quality of a Renaissance workshop picture, one that cannot be attributed to the hand or even the design of any one master. This is readily apparent from the discrepancies in the lighting, the color, the perspective, and the rhythms of its two sides. It was painted in the workshop of Verrocchio — perhaps partly by Verrocchio himself — with the intervention of Leonardo in the angel and the landscape, as a collaborative work involving one or two of Verrocchio's other assistants (one of whom probably was Lorenzo di Credi). With the notable exception of the angel, the picture belongs more to the metallic and somewhat brittle mode of Verrocchio's *Baptism of Christ* than to the fluid, suave style of Leonardo.

The Annunciation had traditionally been set in an enclosed garden or courtyard — the *hortus conclusus* of the Virgin, a symbol of her immaculateness — or in an interior. Here, although the image of the enclosed garden is retained in the low stone wall, the event is enacted out-of-doors before a distant landscape, an innovation undoubtedly due to Leonardo. The humble house of the Virgin is a splendid Renaissance palace, and the lectern supporting the book from which she was reading when the angel approached is standing on a carved marble sarcophagus decorated with antique motives reminiscent of Verrocchio's marble font in the Old Sacristy in the Church of San Lorenzo. The figures comport themselves with the decorum of noble Florentine ladies of the period. Their air of worldliness is a complement to the interest in nature and in classical antiquity, qualities which have replaced the devotional purposes of earlier representations. In its naturalism, its sophistication, and above all in its courtliness *The Annunciation* accurately reflects the tastes of the artistic milieu in which the young Leonardo moved.

4: THE ANNUNCIATION (detail)

A drawing by Leonardo for the sleeve of the angel of *The Annunciation* is in the library of Christ Church at Oxford; and the hair and drapery of the figure, in their shapes, lighting, and rhythmic cadences, are identical with Leonardo's angel in the *Baptism of Christ* by Verrocchio (Slide 2). But even without such proof, the subtle and mysterious beauty of this angel would persuade us that it was painted by Leonardo. He also did the distant landscape and the screen of trees that acts as a foil between the head of the angel and the sky. A similar role is played by the juniper tree in the portrait of *Ginevra de' Benci* (Slide 6), though in the latter there is a more harmonious fusion between figure and landscape.

The winding road that can be seen behind the angel's head is a device which Leonardo has taken from earlier fifteenth-century Florentine painting (though it is ultimately of Flemish origin), and which he was to use again in the background of the *Mona Lisa* (Slide 17). His fondness for it no doubt derived from the fluid, regular motion with which it takes the eye back into space, and from its relationship to the shape of the spiral. A correspondence can in fact be detected between the undulating shape of the road and the oscillating movements of the angel's hair and sleeve.

The lily which the figure is holding — a symbol of the purity of the Virgin — and the sparkling grasses and flowers of the meadow also look as if Leonardo had painted them. They show the same personal, penetrating quality of vision as his early drawings from nature.

5: MADONNA WITH THE VASE (about 1473–1475), wood, 24½" x 18½"
Alte Pinakothek, Munich

Vasari tells us that he had in his collection of drawings certain ones by Verrocchio, "executed with much patience and the greatest judgment, among them being some heads of ladies of noble mien and with elaborately dressed hair, which by reason of their beauty Leonardo was always imitating." This description perfectly fits the head of the *Madonna with the Vase,* as it does the drawing of the head of a woman, perhaps from Vasari's collection, in the British Museum in London. The drawing is by Verrocchio. But the painting of the *Madonna* cannot be attributed with absolute certainty either to him or to Leonardo. It is a workshop picture, like the Uffizi *Annunciation.* The difficulty of determining who executed it is compounded by the fact that it has been extensively repainted, most noticeably in the face of the Virgin and in the shadows around the head of Christ.

Nevertheless, the spirit of Leonardo is felt throughout the picture, particularly in the

Virgin's drapery, whose pirouetting, silken folds recall those of the angel in *The Annunciation,* and in the distant landscape. The restless motion of its peaks — as if nature, in the way that Leonardo looked at it, could never stand still — is ingeniously contrasted to the stately rhythms of the arches flanking the Madonna and Child. Much of the naturalness and liveliness of the picture stems from the interplay between the symmetrical order of the setting and the asymmetrical composition of the figures, particularly the slight inclination of the Virgin's head to the left.

The half-length Madonna and Child is one of the oldest devotional subjects in Christian art. Since the time of Giotto (1267–1337) it had become a means for expressing the tender and affectionate relationship between the Christ Child and His mother, reflecting the striving, which the Renaissance shared with the art of classical antiquity, to make divine figures tangible in human terms. Even the symbols of their attributes came to be shown as naturalistically seen things. It takes us a moment to realize, for example, that the exquisitely rendered crystal vase with the carnation in the lower right corner of the *Madonna with the Vase* is a symbol of the purity of the Virgin.

6: GINEVRA DE' BENCI (about 1478–1480), wood, 16½″ x 14⅝″, National Gallery of Art, Washington, D. C. Photograph courtesy of H.S.H. the Prince of Liechtenstein

"He drew Ginevra, the daughter of Amerigo de' Benci, a beautiful portrait," Vasari wrote of Leonardo; and an earlier writer reports that Leonardo "in Florence made a portrait from nature of Ginevra d'Amerigo de' Benci, which he did with such perfection that it seemed to be not a portrait but the real Ginevra." The daughter of Amerigo de' Benci was born in 1456. In 1474 she married Luigi Niccolini. Judging from the portrait's style, Leonardo painted it some years after her marriage. In about 1490 she was painted again, as one of the attendant women "wearing costumes of the day," as Vasari says, in the celebrated fresco of the *Visitation* by Domenico Ghirlandajo in his series of incidents from the life of the Virgin in the choir of the Florentine Church of Santa Maria Novella. She was, Vasari says, "a most beautiful girl of the time."

The picture has been cut at the bottom; it may originally have contained the hands. Parts of the bodice are repainted; but the head and the landscape are best-preserved passages of any of Leonardo's early works. The figure is seen against a landscape whose hushed twilight reflects her own mood. The shimmering rhythms of the highlights in her hair, of the glistening light on the pool of water, and of the pattern of light filtered through the spiky screens of the juniper tree animate and, by contrast, enhance the beauty of the regular shapes and even tonal transitions in her face. The juniper tree, incidentally, is the clue to her identity. The Italian word for juniper is *ginepro,* which in Roman dialect becomes *genevra.*

The landscape is an instructive example of aerial perspective. "When the leaves are interposed between the light and the eye," wrote Leonardo, "then that which is nearest to the eye will be darkest, and the most distant will be the lightest, not being seen against the atmosphere." He also observed that "in an atmosphere of equal density the remotest objects seen through it, as mountains, in consequence of the great quantity of atmosphere between your eye and them, appear blue and almost of the same hue as the atmosphere itself." The reason for this, Leonardo says, is that "the blueness we see in the atmosphere is not intrinsic color, but is caused by warm vapor evaporated in minute insensible atoms on which the solar rays fall, rendering them luminous against the infinite darkness of the fiery sphere which lies beyond and includes it." As in everything that he did, art and science go hand in hand.

7:   ST. JEROME (about 1480), wood 40⅝" x 29⅝", Pinacoteca Vaticana, Rome

Soon after he arrived in Milan Leonardo made a list of his paintings, drawings, and sculptures, among which there are "certain figures of St. Jerome." The unfinished picture in the Vatican may well be one of them, though Leonardo painted it while he was still in Florence, perhaps taking it to Milan with him. In style and technique it closely resembles the *Adoration of the Magi* (Slide 8). The bald, ravaged head of the saint is identical with a head in the middle of the group on the right side of the *Adoration* (Slide 9).

The picture has been badly damaged. It was found at the beginning of the nineteenth century in a Roman antique shop, where it was being used as a door. The section with the head had been cut out, but was later found in the shop of a cobbler, who had made it into a table top.

St. Jerome is one of the Latin Fathers of the Church and the author of the Vulgate, the translation of the Bible into Latin. His life was divided between scholarship and ascetic practices. While he was living at his monastery in Bethlehem it happened that a limping lion appeared, causing the other monks to flee in terror. But St. Jerome, unafraid, went to the wounded beast and drew a thorn from his paw. In gratitude the lion attached himself to the saint and is always shown accompanying him.

St. Jerome is represented as either a cardinal or a hermit in the desert, meditating, or beating his breast with a stone. The image of St. Jerome as an ascetic penitent had become popular in Florentine painting shortly after the middle of the fifteenth century, as an expression both of a wave of pietism and of an absorbing interest in anatomy. Leonardo's picture is earlier than his systematic studies of anatomy. But the head and torso are superb examples of his understanding of anatomical structure, no doubt as the result of his training at the hands of Verrocchio.

The eloquence and grandeur of the figure are the outcome of Leonardo's ability to correlate the saint's attitude with the emotions expressed in his face. "Man's state of mind," Leonardo wrote, "must be conveyed by means of the gestures and movements of the various parts of the body."

8:    ADORATION OF THE MAGI (1481–1482), wood, 97⅛″ x 95⅞″, Uffizi, Florence

The *Adoration of the Magi* was painted as an altarpiece — a picture to be placed over an altar — for the cloister of San Donato a Scopeto about a mile south of Florence. In the contract drawn up in March, 1481, Leonardo agreed to complete the work in two and a half years. But he only got as far as the underpainting — laying in the contours and the areas of light and shadow in a monochrome tone of umber brown — before he left for Milan in 1482. The monks of San Donato, as we would expect, stopped Leonardo's payments. Later on, a new commission for the altarpiece was given to Filippino Lippi. His *Adoration of the Magi,* completed in 1497, is now in the Uffizi.

The Adoration of the Magi is one of the most popular subjects in Christian art. It is one of the Seven Joys of Mary. The theme is based on the account in the second chapter of St. Matthew's Gospel of the Wise Men from the East who came to pay homage to the newly born King of the Jews. Many other versions of the story were composed during the Middle Ages. In the early fifteenth century the Magi came to be represented as accompanied by horsemen, animals, and an entourage in exotic costumes. This tradition, divested of its pageantry, is the background for Leonardo's elaborate and panoramic composition. In a vast landscape, barren but for a mound of rocks, two trees, and an architectural ruin, the Magi, with crowds in an arc pressing in around them, venerate the Christ Child. Never had the symbolic meaning of the subject — the homage of wisdom to the new faith — been embodied with greater vividness and dramatic force.

Unfinished as it is, the painting brings together in a masterful synthesis the many preparatory studies that preceded it (Figure 5). All elements assume a seemingly natural place around the central group of the Madonna and Child, drawn together by the triangle that is formed by the figure of the Virgin and the two Magi to either side of her, and by the continuation of its two sides in the staircase and in the rearing horse at the right of the large tree in the background. The arc described by the crowd in the foreground and the vertical accents of the trees and the piers of the ruin complete the geometrical framework upon which the composition is built.

9:    ADORATION OF THE MAGI (detail)

The lower right-hand section of the *Adoration of the Magi,* with the figure of the kneeling Magus, a standing figure at the right, and a group of strange, agitated heads emerging out of the darkness, shows two aspects of Leonardo's art particularly well: his technique of modeling with light and shade, called *chiaroscuro* (meaning light-dark), and his fascination with different facial types.

For Leonardo the most important thing about a painting was its effect of relief. "A painting impresses the spectator only when it makes that which is not real seem raised and detached from the background," he wrote. In his own works he achieved this effect by modeling the forms with a single, dark tone before applying color to them. Colors themselves, without differentiations of light and shade, were of no interest to Leonardo. He felt that "nothing about them save their beauty can be admired, and that is not the doing of the painter but of him who made the colors." Although color would have greatly enriched the *Adoration of the Magi,* what is essential in it has been realized. In the underpainting Leonardo has, in Vasari's words, "produced the effect intended." Color would certainly have altered it — perhaps even "spoiled" it.

The most extraordinary thing about the heads in this detail is their range of types and expressions, particularly in the juxtaposition of delicate, young heads and old, gnarled ones. According to Vasari, Leonardo "was so delighted when he saw curious heads that he would follow about anyone who had thus attracted his attention for a whole day, acquiring such a clear idea of him that when he went home he would draw the head as well as if the man had been present." Several such drawings have come down to us, some originally in the collection of Vasari, with heads similar to those in the *Adoration* — especially in the combination of beautiful and ugly faces. Often called "caricatures," they were done less for the sake of the response they might evoke than in a spirit of search for the ultimate in physiognomic types. Just as Leonardo was interested in all species of creatures and growing things, so he wanted to encompass all the varieties of human beings. The only specific remark Vasari made about the *Adoration of the Magi* was that it contained "many beautiful things, especially heads."

10:   THE MADONNA OF THE ROCKS (1483–1486)
transferred from wood to canvas, 78″ x 48½″, Louvre, Paris

On April 25, 1483, Leonardo and his assistants Evangelista and Ambrogio da Predis signed a contract for an altarpiece for the chapel of the Order of the Immaculate Conception in the Church of San Francesco in Milan. The wings, representing music-making angels, were painted by the da Predis brothers and are now in the National Gallery in London. The central panel, *The Madonna of the Rocks,* was painted by Leonardo himself. A second version, commissioned after Ludovico *il Moro* had taken the original from the chapel, was painted by Leonardo and Ambrogio da Predis between 1494 and 1508, and is today also in the National Gallery in London.

The figures in the picture in the Louvre are seen as engaged in a ritual exchange of gestures to which we, as spectators, are directed by the angel at the right who turns his head in our direction and points to the kneeling figure of the Infant St. John. The Virgin draws the little saint gently toward her as he worships the Christ Child, who responds by raising his right hand in blessing.

The legend of a meeting between Christ on his return from Egypt and St. John on his way to the desert to prepare himself for his mission originated in the Middle Ages. In the later fifteenth century, when the Infant St. John — the *Giovannino* — came to be the object of a cult, his meeting with Christ in the forest was a popular subject in Florentine painting. His presence in *The Madonna of the Rocks* is no doubt an allusion to this tradition. Leonardo has placed the group into an immense, dimly lit grotto — a medieval symbol of the Virgin because its crevices and niches offer, as she does, refuge for the faithful. It is perhaps the reason why this is Leonardo's only picture in which the landscape setting is more important than the figures.

Yet they, organized in the form of a pyramid and illuminated from the front, stand out nobly and clearly against the twilight of the cavern. *The Madonna of the Rocks* is Leonardo's first visionary painting. Through a subtle use of *sfumato* its figures take on the magical and mysterious quality of apparitions, as eloquent spirtually as they are optically, a quality that makes them seem both intimate and distant, like visions of the mind as well as of the eye.

11:   THE MADONNA OF THE ROCKS (detail)

Obscured as it is by dirt and coats of yellow varnish, *The Madonna of the Rocks* is nevertheless the consummate example of Leonardo's technical virtuosity. The colors, especially the red and the various yellows of the angel's drapery, have a glowing, resonant translucence. Though clearly illuminated from a source slightly above them to the left, they seem to give forth light rather than receive it. Light itself is rendered with a dazzling range of effects. It strikes the heads of Christ and the angel with full, though gentle, radiance; it skims along the folds of the angel's drapery, and glistens on the grasses and in the hair of the figures; it fades out and comes to life again as the forms move in and out of space; and everywhere it fills the pictorial space with atmosphere. Leonardo uses it with a range of inflections such as he might have produced on the silver lyre he is said to have played for Ludovico Sforza.

The Madonna of the Rocks has both the interplay of line and light characteristic of Leonardo's early works and the emphasis on rendering forms tonally of his mature style. The play of line is most unrestrained in the grasses and flowers growing out of the crevices in the rocks and in the angel's sleeve. In the contours of the heads and of the Child's body, lines turn into threads of light, and they into lines. Graphic and tonal elements perform a game in which their identities become imperceptibly fused. Leonardo's visual exuberance finally extends to the differentiations between the textures of cloth, flesh, hair, rock, or grass, which he represents with such refinement that we sense not only the surfaces but also the substance of things as if discovering them for the first time.

12:   PORTRAIT OF CECILIA GALLERANI, also called LADY WITH THE ERMINE (about 1485), wood, 21¾" x 15⅞", Museum Czartoryski, Cracow

In 1481 the young, beautiful poetess Cecilia Gallerani became the mistress of Ludovico *il Moro.* Leonardo, while he was working on *The Madonna of the Rocks,* painted a portrait of her. A few years later Bernardo Bellincioni, a Florentine who had become Ludovico's court poet, wrote in one of his sonnets that Leonardo has depicted the Duke's lady in an attitude of seeming to listen rather than to speak. His characterization perfectly fits the mood of the

42

portrait. The ermine she is holding with such tenderness is one of the emblems of Ludovico — its name in Greek, *galé,* being an allusion to Cecilia's own last name.

An inscription in the upper left-hand corner of the picture, reading *La Belle Feroniere/ Leonard D'Avinci,* was added about 1800. The background, the left part of the body, and the lower part of the hand have been repainted. But Cecilia's face and the ermine have the articulate anatomical structure and the lustrous surfaces — alabaster smooth, and furry — characteristic of Leonardo's brush.

In the spring of 1498 Isabella d'Este wrote to the Countess Cecilia Gallerani that she would like to borrow her portrait by Leonardo in order to be able to compare it with some portraits by Giovanni Bellini. Cecilia lent her the picture, but only grudgingly. She felt, she said, that it no longer resembled her. But her reluctance could also have been motivated by the fact that it is not only a likeness of her but also an allegorical portrayal of her love for her lord. Leonardo has painted her as if she were "listening" to her thoughts of love while gently caressing the object of her love — the emblematic representation of Ludovico. In 1489 Beatrice d'Este, Isabella's first cousin, had prevailed upon him to give up Cecilia and had become his wife. It would not be difficult to understand Cecilia's hesitation at sending to the Duke's cousin by marriage this memento of her love for him.

In the subtlety of its inflections of tone and shape this portrait, like that of *Ginevra de' Benci* (Slide 6), is matched only by the portraits of Hans Holbein the Younger (1497/8–1543).

13: PORTRAIT OF A MUSICIAN (about 1485), wood, 16⅞" x 12¼"
Biblioteca Ambrosiana, Milan

The *Musician* is Leonardo's only surviving male portrait. It is also the best preserved of all his pictures. Only the face and hair have been completely finished. All surfaces and colors are very close in appearance to the way Leonardo left them, without the effects of later varnishing or repainting that have partly disfigured all his other works in painting.

In its oblique pose and in the motive of the sheet of vellum the *Musician* shows Leonardo's debt to Flemish painting and to the portraits of one of his predecessors as court painter in Milan, Antonello da Messina. A partly effaced inscription on the vellum can be made out as *"Cant . . . Ang . . ."* — *Canticum Angelicum,* the title of a musical composition by Franchino Gaffurio, conductor of the choir at the Cathedral of Milan from 1482 until his death in 1522, and the founder in 1485 of a music school under the auspices of Ludovico *il Moro.* The date of the portrait must also be about 1485, for the modeling and lighting are identical with the handling of the faces in *The Madonna of the Rocks.* It probably represents Gaffurio, and may have been painted on the occasion of the foundation of his school.

The *Musician* coincides in date with the beginning of Leonardo's systematic studies of anatomy and reflects these in its emphasis on articulating with particular clarity the bone structure of the head and the formation of the eyes, nose, and mouth. It is Leonardo's most naturalistic painting and the one that most anticipates the later, though harder and more gleaming, naturalism of Caravaggio (1573–1610).

14:   THE LAST SUPPER (1495–1498), fresco, 13' 10" x 29' 7½", Refectory of the Convent of Santa Maria delle Grazie, Milan

The Last Supper was painted on the commission of Ludovico *il Moro.* In June, 1497, the Duke sent a memorandum to his secretary Marchesino Stanga saying in part that "of Leonardo of Florence it is to be solicited that he finish the work in the refectory." Eight months later Luca Pacioli, the mathematician and friend of Leonardo, in the dedication of his book *Divine Proportion,* spoke of the fresco as completed. Among several eyewitness accounts of the progress of the work, the best known is by the novelist Matteo Bandello, who as a boy had gone to the Dominican school at Santa Maria delle Grazie. "Many a time," Bandello wrote in a book of tales published in 1554, "I have seen Leonardo go early in the morning to work on a platform before the *Last Supper;* and there he would stay from sunrise till darkness, never laying down the brush, but continuing to paint without either eating or drinking. Then three or four days would pass without his touching the work, yet each day he would spend several hours examining it and criticizing the figures to himself. I have also seen him, when the fancy took him, leave the citadel, where he was modelling his colossal horse [the equestrian monument of Francesco Sforza], and go straight to the convent, where he would take up a brush and give a few touches to one of the figures; and then suddenly he would leave and go elsewhere."

The fresco technique does not tolerate such an irregular, eccentric method of working, and this, in addition to the fact that Leonardo was using a medium containing oil and varnish, caused the painting to begin deteriorating almost as soon as it had been completed. Vasari saw it in May, 1566, and reported that there was "nothing visible except a muddle of blots." The mural has been restored several times, and probably looks better now than when Vasari saw it.

Leonardo has chosen to depict the moment following Christ's words: "One of you is going to betray me." The protesting apostles have been organized in four interconnected groups, two on each side of Christ. The composition is held together by the horizontal bar of the table, the three windows in the back, and the perspective patterns of the ceiling and of the panels on the walls, which ensure the regularity of the three-dimensional space in which, as on a stage, the action takes place.

15:   THE LAST SUPPER (detail)

The figure of Christ is both the thematic and the compositional center of the picture. He knows the truth and the inevitability of the words He has just spoken and sits quietly with outspread arms, prepared to accept His martyrdom. "The words are uttered," Goethe wrote in 1817, "and the whole company is thrown into consternation: but He inclines his head, with bent-down look, while the whole attitude, the motion of the arms, the neck, and every thing, seems to repeat the inauspicious expression, which silence itself confirms: Verily, verily, there is one among you that betrays me."

Christ is the fulcrum on which the gesticulating groups to either side of him are balanced. He is not in the absolute center of the composition, however, but slightly to one side of the axis established by the windows behind him. The vanishing point of the perspective construction has been placed just above His head so that He becomes literally the focus of the painting. The round pediment above Him and the foreshortened circular plate between His arms also emphasize and stabilize His central position. The composition not only converges on Him but also, by virtue of His outspread arms, emanates from Him. His arms and head, finally, form a triangle, the shape preferred by Leonardo and after him by all the masters of the High Renaissance style for its ability to establish harmony and unity.

16:   THE LAST SUPPER (detail)

"That figure is most praiseworthy," Leonardo wrote in his *Treatise on Painting,* "which by its action best expresses the passions of the soul," a belief derived from the art of classical antiquity and formulated in Leon Battista Alberti's treatise *On Painting* (1435) by the assertion that the "passions of the soul are made known through the movements of the body." The "movements of the body" — what Leonardo calls "action" — are essentially the same as the rhetorical gestures used by actors to convey the feelings and thoughts of the characters whom they portray on the stage. The apostles in Leonardo's *Last Supper* are the most universally admired examples of dramatic rhetoric in painting.

Leonardo was a ceaseless observer of attitudes and gestures. "When you have well learned perspective and have by heart the parts and forms of objects," he wrote, "you must go about, and constantly, as you go, observe, note, and consider the circumstances and behavior of men in talking, quarreling, or laughing or fighting together: the actions of men themselves and the action of the bystanders, and take note of them with slight strokes in a little book which you should always carry with you."

Goethe shrewdly commented on Leonardo's use of the motion of the hands in *The Last Supper.* "This resource," he wrote, "was obvious to an Italian. In this nation, the whole body is animated, every member, every limb, participates in any expression of feeling, of passion, even of thought. By a varied position and motion of the hands, the Italian signifies: What do I care! . . . This is a rogue! — etc."

He has also left us a memorable description of the apostles shown in this detail: "St. James the Elder draws back, from terror, spreads his arms, gazes, his head bent down, like one who imagines that he already sees with his eyes those dreadful things, which he hears with his ears [for a study of his head see Figure 7]. Thomas appears from behind his shoulder, and, advancing toward the Saviour, lifts up the forefinger of the right hand toward his forehead. Philip, the third of this group, completes it in a most pleasing manner: he is risen, and bending forward, towards the Master, lays the hands upon his breast, as if distinctly pronouncing: Lord, I am not he — Thou knowest it — Thou seest my pure heart — I am not he!"

17: MONA LISA (about 1503–1506), wood, 30¼″ x 20⅞″, Louvre, Paris

Man's most endlessly fascinating adventure into the unknown is not the philosopher's or the scientist's, but one which we pursue every day of our lives: the quest to understand ourselves and others. It is also the most universal subject of art. To a great extent, art deals with the truth that no matter how well we may know others, the self of another remains a mystery. The *Mona Lisa* touches upon this truth more profoundly, or so it would seem, than any other known work of art, and is perhaps for this reason, even more than for its sublime beauty, the most famous picture ever painted.

Leonardo has here used the *sfumato* technique to make it appear that we are seeing the figure through a veil. Light and shadow reveal and also obscure her form. She is both near and remote. Her smile causes her face to come to life, but not to have an identifiable expression. As a human being, too, Mona Lisa is both present and distant. Leonardo has painted not only her image but also the living, intangible personality behind the image.

Mona Lisa was born in 1479 as Lisa Gherardini. In 1495 she married the Florentine merchant Francesco del Giocondo for whom, according to Vasari, Leonardo painted her portrait — although Antonio de' Beatis, who saw the picture in 1517 at Cloux, said that is was painted for her lover, Giuliano de' Medici.

The serenity of her expression is admirably correlated with the repose of her attitude and of her crossed hands. Leonardo has placed her pyramidal form against the visionary landscape below and beyond her in such a way that her presence seems to fill the whole of its vast, strange solitude.

18: ST. ANNE, VIRGIN AND CHILD (about 1508–1510)
wood, 67⅛″ x 50⅞″, Louvre, Paris.

In an account of the travels of the Cardinal Luigi of Aragon, written by his secretary Antonio de' Beatis, we read that "on the tenth of October 1517 Monsignor and the rest of us went to see, in one of the outlying parts of Amboise, Messer Leonardo da Vinci the Florentine, a grey-beard of more than seventy years [he was in fact only sixty-five], the most eminent painter of our time, who showed to his Eminence the Cardinal three pictures," one of which was "the Madonna and Child in the lap of St. Anne." This monumental painting, which is now in the Louvre, is Leonardo's third life-size composition of this subject.

Representations of the Virgin and Child with St. Anne, the mother of Mary, go back to the fourteenth century. The three figures were worshipped as a "human" Trinity, complementing the more remote, "divine" Trinity of Father, Son, and Holy Ghost. Between 1485 and 1510 the cult of St. Anne became widespread — the writer Jakob Wimpfeling went as far as to claim that St. Anne was "overshadowing the fame and glory of her daughter" — as the result of renewed interest in the doctrine of the Immaculate Conception of Mary, the belief that Mary was preserved from original sin from the moment of being conceived by her mother (since 1854 an official dogma of the Catholic Church).

In this painting Leonardo has expressed both the individuality of the three main figures and their oneness as the Holy Family through the masterful control of their movements — what he himself would call their "action." The clear, rhythmic gestures of each flow together in a tightly knit, unified sequence. The stabilizing form of the triangle is used to inscribe the figures not only two-dimensionally but also in space. The group is a matchless embodiment of the balance between action and repose, the momentary and the eternal, the particular and the general.

The background landscape shows no signs of habitation or human presence. It seems to be seen from a distance so great that it appears like a planet. It is a cosmic landscape, an image which often recurs in Leonardo's late drawings and geological studies.

19: ST. ANNE, VIRGIN AND CHILD (detail)

From where did Leonardo derive the radiant, benign faces of St. Anne and Mary? In his *Notebooks* he wrote that "it is no small charm in a painter to be able to give his figures a pleasing air, and whoever does not possess the grace naturally may acquire it by study, in the following way. Be observant to take the best parts of many beautiful faces, whose beauty is confirmed by general consent rather than by your own judgment, for you may easily be in error by chosing faces that bear a resemblance to your own, inasmuch as it would seem that such similarities please us."

Sigmund Freud, in his essay on Leonardo's childhood dream, suggests a more personal origin for the visages of the Virgin and St. Anne. Sir Kenneth Clark has summarized Freud's argument as follows. He "imagines that Leonardo must have spent the first years of his life with his mother, the peasant Caterina; but a year after his birth his father married, and when Ser Piero found that his wife was unlikely to have children, he brought his love child to be looked after by her. In a sense, therefore, Leonardo had two mothers. And it is the unconscious memory of these two beloved beings, intertwined as if in a dream, which led him to dwell with such tenderness on the subject of the Virgin and St. Anne." Freud's suggestion, in Sir Kenneth's view, "explains the apparent nearness in age of the mother and daughter, the strange intermingling of their forms, and their remote, mysterious smiles."

In regard to the smiles, Freud did consider the possibility that connoisseurs of art "will discover something similar in the figures of Leonardo's teacher, Verrocchio, and will therefore not be inclined to follow my deductions." He might also have pointed out that *Mona Lisa* (Slide 17) and *St. John the Baptist* (Slide 20), Leonardo's only extant paintings from the same period as *St. Anne, Virgin and Child,* have similar smiles. Whatever the conscious or subconscious origins of these smiles, they are a general characteristic of Leonardo's late, idealizing style, a symbol, it would seem, of the life of the spirit.

20:   ST. JOHN THE BAPTIST (about 1515–1516), wood, 27¼″ x 22½″, Louvre, Paris

The *St. John* is the only painting that has survived from the last years of Leonardo's life. It was one of the pictures which Antonio de' Beatis saw in Leonardo's house near Amboise in 1517, though it had been painted in Rome a year or two earlier. Disfigured as it is by damage and repainting, it is nevertheless a work of a great beauty and power, invaluable for the insight it gives us into the last stage of Leonardo's evolution as a painter. His interest in what lies behind and beneath appearance — the subordinating of naturalism to ideal, symbolic, and mystical intuitions — reaches its culmination. The chiaroscuro modeling is employed so as to give the figure the character of a vision. It emerges out of darkness but is also about to recede back into it and disappear.

This is not the St. John of the Gospels, the harsh ascetic who announces the coming of Christ, the gnarled, grim figure of Verrocchio's Baptism of Christ (Slide 1). It is a strange, unsettlingly beautiful figure, feminine rather than manly, not belonging to an earthly category of being. His upward-pointing gesture is often found in the angel of the Annunciation, though Leonardo had also used it for St. Thomas in *The Last Supper* (Slide 16) and in the St. Anne of the *Cartoon for St. Anne, Virgin and Child* in London (Figure 11). The gesture signifies mediation between heaven and earth, and was taken by Christian artists from the rhetorical vocabulary of classical antiquity.

It has been said that the *St. John* is the bearer not of a message (the coming of Christ) but of an oracle. Once more, and more subtly than in any of his other paintings, Leonardo has correlated the figure's facial expression with its attitude. Both the saint's smile and his gesture express the aged Leonardo's realization that the principle governing life and creation lies beyond the visible and can be grasped only through symbols. This, it would seem, is the meaning of the picture. As a scientist, a man who deals in facts, Leonardo was surpassed within a few generations of his death. As an artist, a man who deals in symbols, he is immortal.